# The DFC

*I'LL HAVE ONE OF BOB'S BURGERS!!*

## Contents

| | | |
|---|---|---|
|  **Vern & Lettuce** By Sarah McIntyre | | **2** |
|  **Peach de Punch** By Misako Rocks | | **4** |
|  **Little Cutie** By Gary Northfield | | **6** |
|  **Vern & Lettuce** By Sarah McIntyre | | **8** |
|  **Heroes of the Ramp** | | **10** |
|  **Crab Lane Crew** By Jim Medway | | **12** |
|  **Sausage and Carrots** By Simone Lia | | **16** |

---

### MEET THE AUTHOR

**GARY NORTHFIELD**
Creator of LITTLE CUTIE

**LOVES:** watching Bambi, weird music, cheese spread.
**HATES:** car journeys, peanut butter, early mornings.

### MEET THE AUTHOR

**JIM MEDWAY**
Creator of CRAB LANE CREW

**LOVES:** bakewell pudding, puffins and mustard.
**HATES:** the phone ringing, the smell of pet shops and evil dragons.

# VERN AND LETTUCE
### by Sarah McIntyre

**WANTED:**

*Musical Instrument*

Will swap for home-made jumper.

Contact Vern, Flat 6.

KNOCK KNOCK

Hi Vern! I'd like to swap this tuba.

I've had it for ages but never learned how to play.

That's great!

"Here is my size. I'd like to swap for an extra large jumper."

"Wow – that's big! Can I make you a scarf instead?"

"It's a big instrument, so fair's fair."

"I suppose so."

*Later that afternoon ...*

"Here you go."

"It's perfect!"

"That jumper took all my wool! Still, this tuba is ace!"

*More from Vern and Lettuce on page 8*

Peach de Punch
Peach! It's time for your bath!
THUMP!!

Why are you hiding?

Ahh! You're scared of having a wash!
Meow!

OK. Let's do it now.

Meo...w

Peach! Stop that! Don't move! Ouch!

Scrub scrub

Swwwushh!!

Shhhh!

Peach, you smell nice! Nara, why can't you be as clean as Peach?

Meowwn

Oh thanks, Mum!

I need another plaster..

Come on, Sophie. Come and play in the rain with **Little Cutie!!** and me.

I don't want to get my hair wet.

You're a water-bird, silly! Ha Ha Ha Ha Ha Ha Ha Ha

Well I'm different. I don't want to.

You're meant to get wet!

Well you can't sit there all night. This rain will last for ages.

I'll wait

Don't worry – I've got just the thing!

WHOOMP!

Here you go!

It's a bit broken, but it should be OK.

**Panel 1:**
Thanks Charlie.
Now my hair won't get wet.

**Panel 2:**
Aargh! I'm taking off!
HELP!

**Panel 3:**
CHARLIE!
Oh well, at least she didn't get her hair wet.

**Panel 4:**
Fwoomp!

**Panel 5:**
SPLOOSH!

**Panel 6:**
AARGH!
Well, maybe it's a little damp.

VERN AND LETTUCE
BY SARAH McINTYRE
I love my new tuba!
Now I need to learn to play it.
BWAAT.
Oh dear, it must sound very loud downstairs.
THUMP THUMP
Sorry!
BWAAT
Hey Vern! That's too loud! Go and practise somewhere else.

BWAAT.

Argh! That noise!

Let's get out of here!

Wow! It scares moles away!

BWAAT BWAAT

Maybe I can sell the idea to gardeners!

# HEROES OF THE RAMP

Do you have a bike? A skateboard? Some inline skates? Then you could have lots of fun with a ramp. Ask your friends to help!

## THINGS YOU'LL NEED

- A big patch of earth where you can dig (check with a grown-up before you dig)
- A spade
- A helmet
- Some pads for elbows and knees
- A bike, scooter, skateboard or inline skates.

## INSTRUCTIONS

1. Use the spade to make the earth into a small hill.
2. Pat the earth down to make a ramp.
3. Put on your helmet and pads.
4. Zoom over the ramp!
5. See if you can do stunts, like jumps.
6. BE CAREFUL!

# CRAB LANE CREW

BY JIM MEDWAY

Wow!

*The next morning...*

Come on guys. We need to build a ramp!

What are you on about?

It's OK. We're not doing anything else today.

Sounds like fun!

Yes! Come on!

*Soon...*

Here's a spade, and Chris is bringing one, too.

Should we take a wheelbarrow?

We could open a tool shop with all this lot!

Good work, team! Let's start building it up here.
We can take soil from over there.
Three hours later...
We just need to make the top flatter.
I'm so tired!
Me too!
Pass the lemonade, Keely.
Here you go.
What do we do now?
Let's go and get our bikes. We can meet back here. It's so exciting!

I haven't got a bike.
I've got a scooter, but no bike.
I'm getting one for Christmas.
My Dad locked mine up and lost the key.
Just me, then? I'll go and get it.
What about us?
Ten minutes later...
You're back quickly. Where's your bike?
It's got a flat tyre.
C'mon, let's get these tools home.
We'll sleep well tonight.
What a waste of a day!

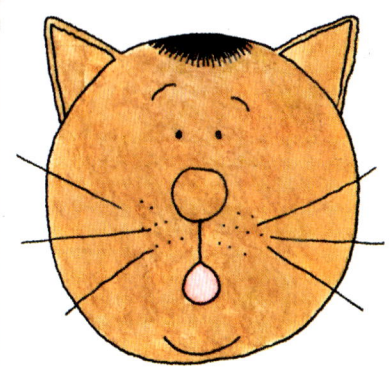

*Next morning...*

Right, Ahmed, let's fix that flat tyre.

Thanks, Mum!

Can't wait to try out the new ramp!

Hi Ahmed!

Woo-hoo!

Ha ha! Room for one more?

# Sausage AND carrots

Simone Lia

"I keep forgetting things, so I'm going to use this notepad to make a list of things to remember."

"Oh no. I've forgotten what I was going to write down."

"Oh that's it! I need to buy a pen to write things down."

"Aargh! I can't write "buy a pen" until I've bought one!"

**Riddle:**
Q. What is the biggest ant?
A. An elephant.

**Joke:**
What do you get if you cross a tiger with a kangaroo?

A stripy jumper!